SHOCK
HORROR

SHOCK HORROR

A Wife's True Story

MARY OXLEY

PARTRIDGE
A Penguin Random House Company

To order additional copies of this book, contact
Toll Free 800 101 2657 (Singapore)
Toll Free 1 800 81 7340 (Malaysia)
orders.singapore@partridgepublishing.com

www.partridgepublishing.com/singapore

Contents

Chapter 1   About myself.. 1

Chapter 2   Fourth Year of Marriage 3

Chapter 3   Feeling Strangulated... 5

Chapter 4   Three is a Crowd 9

Chapter 5   Zorba the Greek 11

Chapter 6   Spanish Holiday 14

Chapter 7   The Garden Shed...16

Chapter 8   Time to Myself.. 19

Chapter 9   Discuss a Separation... 23

Chapter 10   Christmas Day.. 25

Chapter 11   Meeting Begins.. 27

Chapter 12   My Inner Self... 29

Chapter 13   Agents Advice..31

Chapter 14   Getting a Grip... 33

Chapter 15   Doorbell Rings 35

Chapter 16   Conversation... 37

Chapter 17   Rosemary Leaves my Home................................... 39

C h a p t e r 1
About myself

I n the early days of my life my parents were farmers although I spent very little time on the farm. Fantastic memories of those sweet days have never left my thoughts. Mummy seemed to have lots of help. One of the daily helpers name was Mary. In my eyes she kept herself so busy and worked very hard.

I do believe the farm to be extremely work orientated. Let me remind you this is the year 1945 and I was two years old, so all the things that happen on a daily basis and even being at such an early age everything was visual. Each day of the week organized to specific house hold duties, a bit like being in the army. I did not participate of course. I did ask once if I could help clean the silver and I was quickly told I was too young and elbow grease was required. My answer apparently was "where do I find elbow grease?"

Our second member of daily help arrived from Italy and her name was Emmer, a beautiful, very large and delightful person. She became our domestic, living with us full time. I remember her sitting at our refectory table eating enormous plates full of spaghetti. This food was so new to us and mother soon put a stop to that within six months. Emmer's 16 stone was reduced to 12 stone pretty quick. Looking back to those tender years, apart from Mary and Emmer, I had nobody really to talk to. Daddy was very much older than mother by 30 years. He was lovely and showered his wisdom upon me. Once I was sent to boarding school he became distance for a few years.

At four and a half years old I went to boarding school, a lovely convent to start term boarding. I can recall my first day before my journey began about ten miles from my family farm. Porridge was served for my breakfast and my aunt, who was staying at the farm at the time, reminded me many years later how applaud she was when mother scalded me severely for refusing breakfast. The sight of the school trunk with all my personal contents including my teddy bear was making my heart was sink. I felt sick; however we were always dressed beautifully in the uniform colors of black and white. Having my pale blond hair in a bob style, I certainly looked the part in my black blazer edged with white kind of silk, a convent badge stitched so well, white cotton socks, black patent button shoes, and a panama hat to finish the outfit.

I really do believe this was mothers way to the outside world; having her daughter dressed beautifully and on her way to a good education.

As I understand education is cheap; Ignorance is expensive.

C h a p t e r   2

Fourth Year of Marriage

Into the fourth year of marriage, we traveled to our places of work together. Even though it was only a few miles (approx. six miles), running two cars seemed an unnecessary extravagance, so we exchanged two cars. One being my personal and his own car. We felt we were being quite efficient. Saving money makes sense, but to my way of thinking he would not have the hours available to himself to be left to his own deficient, expand his addiction, and it would give me more control of his whereabouts as well as interrupting his hours at home whilst I am at my business and envisaging my dread of what I am going to find today.

The car is a white Mazda 326 with an electric roof and blah, blah, blah; I loved it. The new situation to and from our places of work seemed questionable. At least whilst the novelty lasted, I started to relax and he would always be prompt, prior a phone call of time to pick me up at my salon. On the journey home probably two-three times a week we would call at our local bar and enjoy early doors. I could relax and he could enjoy his whiskey. I felt quite pleased and wondered maybe he now prefers a drink opposed to cross-dressing. Looking back, which was the better of the two evils? All the time I seem to take one step forward and one back.

I told myself time and time again I will not be beaten. I must continue to gather all the strength in my mental ability. It's a constant battle and being very much on my own. I feel I am living two different lives; one being business the other personal.

Often my early door acquaintances would remark that I look miles away and ask are you ok? Yes, only because the skeleton in my cupboard never leaves my mind. I will explain in a later chapter why I refer to friends as acquaintances.

Looking at him across the bar surrounded by his chums, not one of them is ever going to believe who he really is behind closed doors. This well positioned, upper middle class perfect gent was charming to all the females in his sector who often remarked to me what a charming husband you have. If only my husband was so attentive.
Of course he was well practiced and well adapted to all occasions. He achieved this at this level; I will at least give him his due. If only I could take this charming man everyone sees home and have him stay that way. Unfortunately it is not to be.

He is an extremely organized person for instance. Who else would have exact change each morning to collect the daily newspaper seven days a week, fifty two weeks of the year for essential racing news - betting, office hours being seven AM, enabling him to finish a three PM meeting, his chums drinking time. This is the early 80's, but even then his drinking habits had not registered with me even though his pockets were never without extra strong mints.

Chapter 3
Feeling Strangulated

I now have three major issues: cross-dressing, drinking, and daily betting. If I confronted him about his drinking his answer would be happy days are here again. I realize I am side tracking slightly from the main point of this book, but I need you to get the full picture of how clever they plan each day to be the closet queen. I have not mentioned his age, born 1930 under the sign of Taurus; a sign well know for split personalities. One funny incident was on a Sunday afternoon. The doorbell rang and it was the gardener wanting to discuss matters of work for the following week. Oh dear, what a shame, he still had nail polish on from Saturday evening. All he could do was wear a pair of gloves, and this was rather a hot summers day. I never asked the excuse, It was just another one to me. These were the risks he took continually and never having friends calling without prior notice.

I began to feel slowly but surely strangulated by what is happening to me as a person. I realized how I used to laugh a lot, and that I was not me anymore. My quality of life was slowly diminishing. I think he begrudged me as a women; the more I looked after myself and the better I looked the worst the situation. Having said that, that is my tool which many years later became my salvation one thing he can never be is me.

Just when I felt I was getting a grip on things, retracting back to a nail incident, my mind went into gear. It appears on the face of it only nail polish, no signs of cross-dressing on the Saturday afternoons whilst I am still at business or started to secretly cross-dress on Sunday afternoon thinking I wouldn't be home, as I often went visiting antique shops, my favorite hobby, and where was his attire of course? My guess was the garden shed, which he kept locked for reasons of safety, or so he said.

So now I must keep my peace and start a careful approach since he had not reformed. How and when does all this take place? What I hate about all this nonsense is the deceit and deception. It would be better to admit everything and say, "Yes, I cross-dress. I have no intention of stopping." At least I'd would know where I stood in this marriage, if you can call it that.
But no, he enjoys being a closet queen. Obviously that's the buss, and of course adrenaline rush of the "I am a naughty boy" scenario.

As I explained earlier, I have a dressing room. Obviously I do not wear all my clothes all the time, which are top of the line designer, and looking closely to my horror signs of wear and tear, make up marks and my stretched under-wear tights worn. How could anyone, particularly your husband, do that? In fact, there was very little that had not been got at. How could he do such a thing and hurt me so much? I felt physically sick and getting so concerned as to what sort of person am I living with.

I now feel I have to start being a detective to get to the bottom of this obsession.

Apparently the cross-dresser closet queens love to take selfie photos, so I decided I need to find such items for evidence. Things like taking his own pictures to admire himself only he can admire. I wondered how will I get the pleasure of been shown the frock horror in actual print. When this appears, and it will, it will take all my energy to say absolutely nothing only to sit and plan and become the secret partner, with a future towards a separation or even better a divorce, no matter how long it takes I am not a revenge person, however mess with my hard earned wardrobe and personal belongings, then things get serious. He is totally unaware of my perception of the closet queen I am enduring.

Could it get any worse? Well- readers read on.

During the short journey home from work he asked me a favor, saying it was totally up to me as to whether I agreed or not. First was he going to come clean at last. I replied with, "Ready to compromise? What is this favor?"

"Well, do you remember meeting a very nice young lady a few months ago?"

My reply, "I certainly do as a matter of fact, we got along rather well?"

"She is returning to England and would rather not stay with her parents, as they are too restricting. Could she stay with us? It would only be for a short time, maybe two to three weeks. She would be company for the Pekinese during the day and she's a pleasure to have around. Like you she dresses well, glamorous and all that."

"As long as she understands I am out all days of the week, as long as she looks after my home and helps with meals I cannot see a problem." It was agreed and arrangements were duly made. Of course, my thoughts go further. Maybe at long last I can at some point discuss my situation with trust and in privacy in my home. I felt somewhat relieved that my burden would hopefully be lifted.

So the house was prepared. My dressing room was altered to give her wardrobe space to make her as comfortable as possible. We invited friends along for dinner to introduce everyone as they will be around at the different places where we socialize for her stay and no longer, owing to a long awaited holiday planned with two other friends to visit Spain.

The first week went so well, I started to relax and smile more and evenings were so pleasant and full of long dinners, nice wine, and music. Progressing into the second week I felt safe to be able to discuss matters that has been on my mind for such a long time. As the weekend approached I gathered up the courage to bear all to find the opportunity was not easy as my husband seemed always in the way. How frustrating this became, being as my gun was loaded and bursting at the seams. Looking back, how ironic it was that I could not find the right moment for such a serious discussion. Once again the chat was put to bed.
I am a great believer in fate, and that hand certainly not to be played.

Nearing the end of week two the closet queen husband started his holiday leave before mine. Being self-employed, those options do not apply. You take a week here and there when possible if you're lucky. So now I have the car and the independence to travel to my place of business without him, leaving at home to his own devices plus the company of my female visitor, to whom I trusted to take care of matters (I.e. preparing dinner, dog walking, etc.). Not a lot to ask in return for my hospitality.

Chapter 4

Three is a Crowd

Nearing the end of my husband's friend's stay I left my business earlier than expected, around 3 p.m. having a lot to deal with (packing)). It was a relief to have two hours at hand. I did not phone to say I was on my way. I had no reason to do so. As I approached my house all seemed quite quiet. I parked my car in the driveway and got out of the car thinking nothing unusual, except the Pekinese who was being quiet. I enter the front door called, "Hello I am home early!" "Hello!" Not a sound. I continued to make myself heard as I places my bag and brief case down. I looked in all the rooms downstairs. My heart was starting to pound as I sensed something wrong. I approach the stairs going up still calling, "I am home!" I step on the top landing and move towards the master bedroom. I tapped on the bedroom door and behold my guest and my husband are well. Let's call it the hornets' nest, for a better word. They made no attempt to move. I could not believe my eyes. I moved away from the bedroom door sat on top of the stairs in total shock. I remember saying in a loud voice, "You?! Husband, you do not know what you have done to me!" Both have crucified my being, limb by limb. I remain sitting on the stairs hurt, gutted, and speechless. Still no movement. Unbelievable. The dogs are never allowed upstairs, this time they sat with me as if they knew my terrible pain.

At this point I slowly went down the stairs to the kitchen and sat numb. Half an hour later the two eventually appeared looking like the cat got the cream. I look at the them, at a loss for words. The trust I had with this female visitor was gone. My mind is racing so fast. I am married to a closet queen, drinker, gambler, and now, adulterer. I never thought this possible.

There is certainly no more room in my house for three people. This is my house. Pack up your female friend this minute and leave. You want each other, therefore, you can have each other, and tell him not to forget his make-up. On that note her face was a picture, realizing she has more than she had bargain for.

With no more ado, they gather themselves and left. I do not know where nor do I care. I am too in shock to go down that road.

A holiday pending a husband I never want to see again. At this moment in time the best thing I can do is retire to bed, if that is feasible, and think of my pending holiday. What a relief to have that to hold onto, as I am sure my husband will return sooner or later. However I am a strong women and I will put on a face as if nothing has happened. I cannot un-do what is past, my life is more important. I will move on and he will go eventually.

I still have to deal with my business tomorrow. That is what I am married to.

Chapter 5
Zorba the Greek

This person called a husband - how many hats can one wear? Cross-dresser, drinker, - gambler,-cross-dress and now philanderer. Surely there cannot be five. Later in my book we will find that out. However, going back to the holiday vacation arrangements being to holiday with another couple. The female just happened to be his secretary. I assumed her to be rather good at her job. During the holiday I gathered from her own words she is unable to type. The penny should have dropped with him being very keen to have her join our holiday company.

We all spent a very enjoyable evening at the airport hotel, having few drinks after dinner. We never mentioned the incident, or rather drama, even though it came up in the conversation of her. Wear will stay with me for a very long. The moment of - my energy will find a solution and certainly will not interfere with my long awaited break; The closet queen is behaving as nothing has happened and seemed to be void of all conscience relating to his misdemeanor.

The four of us had a villa next door to each other. We all part company to address our accommodations. I need to un-pack - as women do we like to be organized. We hang our clothes and change for the Spanish weather. It's so wonderfully warm. Its mid afternoon and we are all to meet on the shared patio for drinks. Three of us are in shorts and tank tops. O.K. Where is closet queen? He duly arrives dressed as Zorba the Greek. Of course it is O.K. We are on an island and its hot -how and when did he think this one up boggles your mind. We all remarked effeminately different. He thought the remark very amusing. My thoughts were very different. Selfish to the end, he is the only person on the planet and seems to have no regard for me. He knows I know the look he is portraying is a slight towards the closet queen. He is safe in so much he has got me under his thumb knowing. I will not be humiliated in front of our company. However, let it go for the time being only. Nobody will think differently.

As the week progresses, I suggested we hire a jeep to tour this beautiful island and see the beaches, find eating places, enjoy the island, and try the local aperitif. How ironic neither my lady company nor my husband are remotely interested., So do we sit all day looking at each other? I do not think so. The husband of our company agrees. That's settled. The husband andmyself depart. We walk into the village and hire the jeep to set off for a wonderful relaxing day. We had a good laugh saying they do not know what they are missing.

Him being such excellent company, this was for me just what the doctor ordered, In fact a godsend for the whole week. Now we have a jeep and the two of us can shop, buy food, local alcohol, and barbecue most evenings - this being my best part of the day. Fantastic.

However, I get the vibes that the two left behind during the day?, Maybe not so.

Plutonic as they were portraying, I am pretty quick at picking up mannerisms.. Looking at her husband nothing seemed to register, or is he just turning a blind eye. This interests me as she has no knowledge of previous events. Thinking to myself, "Join the queue, make a fool of yourself," I feel a lot better. Marvelous. Carry on

Chapter 6

Spanish Holiday

Although Zorba the Greek seems mild in his mind, he is cross-dresser. A disguise to others, My marriage has become celibate and has been for a long time and owing to his morbid behavior, you cannot blame me. I now find him repulsive. It would seem he is addicted to the females he tries to emulate. Seduce them and copy. He has the charm to achieve. He gets what he wants every time. I will give him that credit.

It would appear to me the frock horror syndrome produces stimulus to the penis, so Zorba the Greek is on his own with an attractive female to himself for most part of a sunny day. I am not a male today. He really believes he is, for a few hours, a woman actually and what do they do? Play as no penetration can happen, unless we have a toy box. I feel so naïve and thankfully, normal.

I do recall there was definitely signs of make-up or the smell of self tan showing. Not a sign of body hair. Obviously well prepared for Spanish sun, as mentioned in past chapters the lipstick saga being enough for my tastes. I was so grateful for the holiday. It opened my eyes wider than ever. My thoughts are now to work towards and end my life with this person.

On our return home, I feel hopeful my personal life may be taking a turn for the better, having had a relaxing week away from business. Sun tans helps tremendously. More confident this philandering are just a game to him and not serious affairs, this does not excuse his appalling behavior. Having been through two divorces, a third is imminent. When the time is right financially, with enough evidence to clean him out, and remove his comfortable home which I have created.

We had been home a few weeks now after the holiday. The holiday began to wear off somewhat. However, the unexpected news, and the last thing I expected to hear from him,

"S it down -consider what I am about to disclose. I hope you will be surprised and back me up." the charm is on and it rubs off me like a piece of soap, however it still hit me with this great surprise. "I have been offered promotion I will have three months to settle in find a house so on so forth, yes?"

I am listening half heartily with my mind on two levels. No I will not be joining you. He's so sure I would jump at a change of life. Quite right, I am ecstatic to see the back of you. Please take the three months and we will take it from there, now he is thinking of me? Three months on my own, more like too long to be without a frock, to return home on a two weekly basic, was agreed.

This gave me ample opportunity to find his secret wardrobe (I. e. the garden shed always locked) That has bugged me for a long time. One thing stands in my way, where is the dame key? Before his departure, I enquire, "Does the gardener need anything that I do not have, such as the key?" "That is all taken care of." Ok, at that point I made no more of the shed or the key.

Chapter 7

The Garden Shed

What jogged my memory on this issue was my cannon camera was not where I always keep it. I needed the camera a.s.a.p. for my business tomorrow. I ask the question, "Before you leave any idea of the were about of my camera is?"

His reply (all lies of course), "It's at my office. I will see you have is back before I leave, do not worry." Low and behold he goes straight into the garage, where there is a kind of a tall boy with lots of tiny draws. I am listening to all the rummaging kind of noise. I am in the kitchen window, watching him head down the garden and into the garden shed, on his approach back to the garage with the camera well hidden. No doubt it will appear tomorrow. I am relieved about the camera. I also have a good idea where to find the shed key and be able to disclose frock horror all that has been hidden from me for such a long time.

They give their own game away by over protecting the naughty boy syndrome. I think he even gets a buss out of hiding the shed key- pathetic that is all I can say.

I did retrieve the camera plus apologies for the use. Without more questions I thank him, but where is the film? The camera is empty. At my office it will be replaced forthwith.
I cannot wait for his departure to be given such an opportunity to find who I am really married to.

The day arrived. I drove him to the station in plenty of time to make sure he got on that train, crossing my fingers or the train to be on time, so he would board to his seat instead of straight to the bar I just waved goodbye with a sigh relief.

The time of day is mid-afternoon in mid-winter and I need to get home before dark, so its foot down. I arrived, parked the car straight into the garage and used the car lights to address the tall boy. Now let's find the illusive key. I do not even know what it looks like. There are keys in every drawer, but time is on my side. I try them all, making sure they are were returned as found. It was getting cold and tomorrow is another day, fortunately a Sunday. This could not be better.
Sunday morning, around 7.a.m. in a dressing gown I shut the Pekinese indoors. I approached the shed door. My hand was shaking. With a bunch of keys in hand, hoping to get a fit it seemed forever. Luck is on my side, beautiful. I opened the door and closed it behind me. I turn around, and it's here at this point I'm totally speechless.

The full Monty? --A transvestites? Paradise? Un-believable; bras, suspenders, bottles of water, balloons, sanitary towels, piles of photographs, more clothes than I own, and make-up enough for a year. The state of the place is in says this has been going on for many a year. Certainly before my time and long before. Wigs, all worn and un-washed in all colors; long, short, you name it's here. It is so disgustingly untidy

I do not want to touch an item. Having said that, all the photographs will be kept in my safe keeping. My camera, my film, and therefore they belong to myself. I need something after this experience to work on, the court doors.

I quickly left, locked the shed, and returned the key. On doing so I noticed a second key that was a replica of the same. I now process a key, the day can only get better even the mere sight made me feel sick. Thinking I am married to this under hand moron, also the fact I have no one to confide in.

Still in my dressing gown wondering what to do with myself, I decided to sit in my sitting room a room which I designed mainly all soft pinks-creams.

This is not going to get the better of me. I have a good hand to play with when the time is right and at that moment the phone rings. It's him checking if I am ok. He remarked I sounded tired. My reply was correct, what I would have liked to have said was, yes, tired of you big time.

The photos plus the key will be put in a deposit box at my bank. By the way I have always kept a daily diary religiously. Why? Keep a diary and it will keep you. It did.

C h a p t e r   8

Time to Myself

I admit I did find it extremely tiring keeping the house plus my career together. During his absence, even visits of two weekly routine arrivals, he always took care of the weekly shop, the cleaning the house and so on. After all that is a women's domain. During the three months of his coming and going out of the blue arose a neighborly dispute, which my solicitor to his amazement saying they are harder to resolve than a divorce, but you did? Little did he realize at the time he would be dealing with my husband's divorce against myself at some point in the future.

I feel the time has come to move on. Without the closet queen breathing down my neck, time has been given to me. I wanted to sell the house, lease my business and take a year out. If I do not grasp this time given my life will not change. I cannot contemplate a future as it has been, he is not going to change. What the shed has revealed to me made me feel very unsafe and unhappy. My quality of life belongs to me and nobody has the right to take that away.

Taking a long look at our house, over the past nine months what I have spent in terms of time and money, it's a heart breaking move. Nothing is as awful as living with a person I no longer know. I do not need advice from so called friends, I make the decisions.

I am sure he was so sure the house would not sell. It was not the house that concerned him, it was the Pandora box that will explode his years of the closet queen. His first wife left him and the second is on the way, meaning myself. So back to the house sale. Get this one over price and sit tight, the property will not sell for a long time if ever. Definitely Do not put up a sale board, a photograph in the estate agents window. I will agree to that. Once again it is all about him, self-centered to the bitter end. I personally have a good feeling about the house.

To cut a long story short, the estate agent called to tell me I have a lady viewer. That quick? We were on the market for two weeks only. Not only did she buy the house, but all the contents, including the furniture. That left me with eight weeks to move and find a new place to live. I am a great believer in fate, so if this has gone so well the next move will also. Giving the husband the news was met with a long silence. The shed was not mentioned, but all that concerned my buyer was the size. Luck being on my side, my quality of life is beginning to turn.

Financially I have a dilemma: Do I share the sale or dump the closet queen? Very tempting, as I now hold the reins, but remember he has no knowledge of my findings. This was too good to let go. For the time being I will keep things under wraps, after all he does have his uses.

The road now is to find a new life home. The question is the number one location, with number two in mind with cash available. I feel successful, and in no time at all what I never thought of could be mine. I am in the market to put in an offer. Two weeks and a phone call to say it is yours, unbelievable. I was so excited I could hardly keep still. I want to tell the world. Only there was my husband, my excitement was soon smashed, would his response be dire because we are going to live in an apartment shared with three other tenants? My answer is buying me out and go your own way. It's that simple. Down goes the phone and silence is golden. Excellent, he never did view the apartment or ever take any interest. The ultimatum was more than he could cope, manage, whatever.

Eventually he moved in. Thinking back it was all meant to be. Why did things did not improve? His cross-dressing as closet queen hiding behind closed doors, his real dream to walk about as a women, so now the question is do I mind if he dresses, using the dark nights for walkabouts?

"If I am so convincing as a women, do you think anybody will question you are my wife?"

My answer, "I could not care less if you have the problem, I do not --at least whilst you are cross-dressing the whiskey bottle is left alone."
"One incidence, having been walking about, I must look convincing I actually got a wolf whistle!"

My answer, "That is all I need to hear, bully for you. I just hope nobody recognized you."

His reply, "That your opinion. I look far too good."

I really could not care less what he got up to. I have a new home, a fresh start, a new era and my philosophy being take all the opportunities that are put in front of you. Do not listen to other so called friends, as they will only mislead. After all who are they to give advice not knowing you have a skeleton in the cupboard. They may also be harboring one too. Who knows, you only have to mention the word divorce and everyone backs off. Why? It rocks their boat, the only person I trust is myself.

C h a p t e r 9
Discuss a Separation

I have given myself a year out from business. Time for me to put my new home together, and without his interest. His main interest is ether to take his promotion or discuss a separation. I gritted my teeth hoping the later.

But no, seeing the comfortable home I have achieved, his decision to give the promotion a miss. Put your feet up at my expense and take all the glory. The question pending, we both know you are a closet queen. Where are your hidden secrets? Whilst you have been working away have you replenished, keeping the house and keeping down at my expense? If that is the case you owe me big time. He is very tight with the purse. Rather than part, he admits all is under the spare wheel. How underhanded can one get?

I being fully aware of my findings in the shed, it would be impossible to hide all under a spare wheel. I have to keep that one to myself. Why cover up, constantly, knowing he cannot keep me in the dark any longer. Also I am too ashamed and too loyal to everything to allow anyone into the horrific dark happenings inside my marriage.

It's getting to that time of year nearing Christmas. I know my inner thoughts tell me this will be the last one together. To make the most of it will get me through. This situation is impossible to carry on. My quality of life is nil and our new home seems to have given him an idea that he can carry on regardless; that I will not be moving for many years to come. All his water holes and chums are near to walking distance. His afternoons are free to cross-dress. Selfish isn't the word because to him I do not exist. It would seem only when it suits him to be seen together, looking like the perfect man and wife, to hear yet again what a charming husband I have. That's his game to charm the ladies, but like the flies versus the web, after he caught me, there were plenty more he has to copy. Ladies seem to drop at his feet. He is really sizing you up with his charm to keep your attention from another look at his wardrobe.

We have been settled in our new home approximately six months, he decided to return to his old office and not to take the promotion. A big disappointment which could have solved a delicate situation, meaning the marriage could have faded gracefully.

I am now in my early forties, too young to sit at home pondering. So with no more ado, I have lots of ideas, enthusiasm, and money available. I have nothing to lose and only my ability to succeed. What more receipt do you need only to believe in one's self. Failure dilutes me. I must have an energy gene. People do remark that they envy my strength and energy which I did not realize that potential inside of myself, as I never get applause from the husband other than, I wish I could look like you are so lucky. Keeping the face and bottom up, nothing to do with luck pal, discipline together with routine every day of your life and, you will never be a women. You were born male. Accept the facts, and stop this ridicules imitation.

Chapter 10
Christmas Day

B y this point I had established my career. New premises, excellent location; for me completing new era felt so refreshing. I am feeling in full control of myself as a person and better able to handle my living nightmare.

Let's get back to Christmas Eve. Having ordered a fresh turkey, which I duly carried home. I ventured to my apartment still carrying the turkey and opened the front door expecting help, and what do I find? My husband flat out paralytic on the floor. My thoughts are, cross-dressing upsets that much? He was drunk. It never occurred to him that his wife would have liked to have joined his little party early doors. Just for a moment I felt so neglected. I went into my kitchen opened the second story window and threw the turkey. All I heard was the splat. I felt so much better. Christmas day can look after itself and so can my guests on Christmas day. Once you get past caring, apart from my business life, I feel once again very alone.

I continued my planed evening. I went to the cathedral for midnight mass and it's the one time I am able to wear my favorite fur coat. It's so warm and perfect the church can be rather cold. To my amazement, my husband is rallying round and going to escort me to church. More to the point to let everyone see what a gentleman I have.

Midnight mass so beautiful. I sat with lovely people wondering if they harbor a skeleton in their closet as well. Surely, I am not alone and silence is golden, at lease mine is for the time being.
I felt concerned for my work and for my well-being, and recommend an agent to call making an appointment, to visit me personally. The agent lived within a 20 miles and guaranteed total privacy. With arrangements duly made at my private office.

I arrive at the time of appointment feeling anxious about meeting a total stranger. I have got this far so see it through, and I started wondering what sort of person I am going to meet. At that moment the door opened. We both looked at each other. I wasn't sure what he expected to encounter. Surprised to say the least, a blonde suited, authoritative image; surly this is not the person I have an appointment with. I immediately put him at his ease, directing the two of us to my private office, I have a positive feeling all will be resolved and help is here for me at long last.

Chapter 11
Meeting Begins

Where do I begin to try and put my situation in a nutshell? All of a sudden I felt like I was back at school. Having such a lot to say I seem lost for words and still feel ashamed that I find myself in such a position. The agent has given up his time and travelled 20 miles, but I find myself unable to disclose everything. He obviously understands my dilemma and immediately gives me the encouragement I desperately need, without becoming a pathetic naive individual.

"If it will help you, I am a cross dresser and I represent in my area around 250 cross dressers, so please relax. You are not on your own," he said to me.

"So, are there other women suffering the same way?"

He did explain that most couples sort out their differences, many taking the path of, "if you can't beat them, join them". Bearing that in mind with financial things, children, etc. Unfortunately, the man does not show this side until later on in a marriage. Even though the signs are there, the wife turns a blind eye, or buries her head in the sand, waiting for the fancy cross-dress night at the local bar. The dark side of the male will start to show. He will of course state it's not my scene, however he will be more than willing to attend the chance to cross-dress as a women and be seen. This will no doubt enlighten his penis, and may be that enhances lifts that particular couples sex life. For me it has strangulated me, destroyed our marriage, created abuse, domestic violence and heavy drinking and they see it as normal behavior. You take the wedding ring all in good faith, with a future of normality. He posed the question, but unfortunately, we do not really know a person until we live together. My marriage must be the worst scenario, he cross-dress, drink heavily, gambles, is a philanderer, and queen.

C h a p t e r 1 2

My Inner Self

How do I feel within myself?

After that meeting I went home with a spring in my foot and feeling like I had won the lottery so I decided to call at my favorite water hole. Early doors now being unusual for me I just felt like celebrating all to myself, something I never normally do. I approached the club bar in the beautiful five star hotel I hesitate as I pondered for a moment. A women on my own, do I feel comfortable having a drink? Approaching the bar I could hear familiar voices, low and behold who should be standing at the bar, you've guessed it, the husband. Surprised somewhat to see me at this time of day he offered me a drink. I declined, it was hardly 11:30. He was now under an obligation to introduce his wife unless it suits him I do not exist. His drinking chums faces told the story, I duly left him with egg on his face. I walked home, only a ten minute walk away from my apartment and smiling for once.

Feeling very secure he will not be Rosemary this evening, I escaped another cross-dressing, owing to his drinking until mid-afternoon. Having had a most informative day, far more enlightening today than yesterday, I knew I could cope so much better. Over the next few weeks, husband/ Rosemary noticed a difference in my attitude towards him. He thought I have come to terms with his addiction. It is a great feeling to be in control of one's self. It is only a matter of time. My diary is filling slowly but surely. Cross-dress all you want, do the selfie bit; make a mockery of our marriage. the question is why carry on with such a situation, even the inevitable of a divorce is a nasty business at best, financial costs, facing friends and answering their curiosity. I keep declining that route, keeping my business afloat was my priority because my quality of life is what matters. Living under this umbrella day-to-day you lose sight of how your life should be.

People see me as a strong women, never believing I would contemplate odious appalling behavior managing a marriage of horror for approximately fifteen years.

Mary Oxley

Chapter 13

Agents Advice

My agent informs me of 250 members, who require to shop for their addiction. My new business is doing reasonable well, having a marketing ability a one to two percent of 250 clients we hold all the criteria of a very large stock. Wigs to suit all, make-up, etc. My business will extend to fit this market gap. This will be word of mouth, giving them security for shopping.

It was not long before all walks of life visited. My staff were given professional training. We are there to help and serve, not to be upset by gender. To address the situation, specific hours were put in place. All our new clients were charming, interesting and entertaining, strange as it may seem. The general conservation my "wife" understands, making me feel as a wife. Who is right and who is wrong? I need to keep a grip, but no one knows of my dilemmas. Why do I get so upset in my personal life? My explanation is simple, my marriage vows became a sham. I was taken big time. Being a very honest straight person, that hurts.

Even to this day and all the case histories, I find it difficult to understand. I am not a judge and have no right to stand in judgment. I feel very proud

I was in a position to help cross dressers, even though my situation is still dire. Looking back on 20 years on my personal life they became my life-line. The time they gave me as clients was so positive in helping me to overcome a difficult nearly impossible situation.

Chapter 14

Getting a Grip

My personal life did eventually open to one or two special clients. Having earned their trust and diplomacy I started to feel at ease and not be ashamed which I should never have felt. After all I was dealing with another person's problem taking it all on board as if it were mine. Why do I have to burden a loyalty to keep face. The big lesson for me is never be a people pleaser, the innocent victim being myself is the sufferer.

I decided to invite a couple for dinner. Two guys come dressed to kill and are thrilled to enjoy what they love to do. Ok, no questions asked. They have no idea my husband Rosemary will be revealed. I am well prepared for the unknown. It has to be organized without any repercussions. In other words what I do in my home stays in my home. What I have in mind is so repellent, I offer to do Rosemary a professional make-over. Why? To save my professional image, not wanting my guests to envisage a clown.

Once again I feel it reflects upon myself, even in this situation. Madness in itself, nearly a case of cannot beat them, join them only as long as dinner lasts. I enlighten Rosemary of what is affront. He puts down the whiskey glass, and his reply? Fantastic, at last you are beginning to understand, a brief moment, what you are prepared to live with me as a women in disguise.

This is my future. I do not think so selfish to the end all about Mr. me. Or is Mrs. Me? Now we are ready, she has never looked this good. Even I am impressed, meaning my work not him. Let's keep in mind my guests are clients. I actually hate being under this umbrella, I somehow need to show my ability even at this level. I question myself why do I need to go to such lengths, but I have no answer. What is staring me in the face is sick and upsetting and trying to destroy me as a women. I cannot wait to see how the evening will go.

Chapter 15

Doorbell Rings

The doorbell rings and the door opens as guests arrive, disguised in large coats and boots. They put on high heels and check their make-up. When the girls are ready, they adjoin to the sitting room. I offered them drinks, saying please relax.

Rosemary was upstairs too nervous to appear, which gave me the time to explain my well-kept secret. This was my worst moment, why should this be? Looking at my guests dressed to kill, they certainly have not let me down: cocktail dresses, high heels, full make-up stockings, and wigs in auburn color. I'll give credit where credit is deserved. A lot of trouble had been made, my next move was to introduce my husband as Rosemary. Rosemary entered the room, with first words "join the club". No handshakes, instead they gave cheek kisses. Carry on do not mind me, after all I am now just the hostess. The evening went as well as could be expected under this bazaar umbrella, the cooking of food being my forte, and of course wine helped.

Sitting at my table enjoying the dinner I realized I no longer exist. In fact I felt quite uncomfortable, here I am sat at the table with three males dressed as women. I have brought this upon myself. Quite honestly I feel sick to my stomach, wishing I had not created the evening. Well it was too late for those thoughts.

Let me explain. As good as the thing they can imitate, a real woman, it just does not come off like make-up and clothes no matter how good, how much is spent, there is still a penis, testicles, heavy hands, hairy arms, Adams apple, and beard shadow. Your sex is male and all the above mentioned to name, but a few of you proving you cannot become even a temporary women with success, sorry guys. Tell me the point of all this. There has to be one to risk losing your family and the respect of normal friends.

Still sitting at the table I can only asses the picture as frock horror in reality. My guests personalities are somewhat changed. The conversation was all about marriage break downs, creating financial problems, becoming an outcast to normal society, and mostly behaving behind closed doors. Thinking back to the agent informing me of 250 members in my county, you would think, why do we not see cross dressers in our everyday walk of life? This is the 80's and society is not ready and in my opinion will never be. The evening has certainly been an eye opener, the conclusion is or seems to be to hell with anybody who does not wish to understand their dilemma I call it down right selfish, would they except their wife to cross-dress as a man. I do not think so.

Finally the evening is over. All three kiss each other. I had to turn away. To hell with how I felt, after all I am the real woman. Tomorrow I will still be that real woman and it's a great feeling to be one's self and not living a life in disguise. The evening was a success. I can move on with my loyalty is fading, which has been my downfall.

Chapter 16

Conversation

During dinner, as I mention earlier, my voice was not being heard, however I had to ask a question which has bugged me for a long time. When did this cross-dressing start, being as their ages are now late fifties nearing sixties. A fancy cross dresser was put on at a local venue, men to cross-dress as women and best look wins a prize. Wives and girlfriends all approve, after all it's only a bit of fun. They would at this time in their lives be maybe in their late twenties. This is not the first time to wear ladies clothes, the closet queen has an opportunity to be seen dressed outside his well hidden world. Signs of showing the dark side which you did not know existed. The worst scenario, the female helped put him together for that fatal event.

Why would any sound male want to wear high-heels, make-up, false boobs, shave their legs, stockings and suspenders (his favorite item). I notice how well he could walk in those heels. Really, another valid point, women do not have a desire to cross-dress male, what would the husband think of that? My guess was not a lot, I am not prepared to go down that road. Though it is tempting just to get a reaction to see how it feels for him, the shock and horror. It's too one sided to contemplate, a very disturbing personality, even crazy, maybe. It could cause domestic violence in certain cases, of which I have memories and the scars.

In my experience, For what it's worth, he seems totally convinced that to enjoy playing female is quite normal and harmless. Why not cross-dress as the bride and show to all at the church and let us all know who you really are and let the wife be aware of frock horror, love and marriage? Stop kidding yourself, the female is very astute, your secret will rear its ugly head sooner or later.

Strangely enough, early on in our marriage a well-respected professional male came across to me and said you are married to a very funny chap, not understanding where such a remark could come from. What alerted him to feel the need to tell me that? I was married to a very strange man before any of his hidden "talents" surfaced. It was a remark I will never forget, strange being the operative word, the dinner females dressed in disguise, kissing each other on their first time meeting. If they are gay that's at very least tolerable, but this is insane.

I am now well assured that Rosemary has no regard for me as his wife, a trophy on his arm to all outsiders with all loyalties forgotten. It's time for me to rid myself of this burden I have carried for so long. I do have someone in mind, a chance I should have taken a long time ago. One can only try, and in my case I feel totally justified to take my next move. I am long overdue to encounter an affair. I felt this is not revenge my heart has always been where I am about to take myself. Feeling very confident and rather excited, I disclose my feelings to Rosemary, as always my honesty is foremost and she replies, ok whatever. You will never leave me.

My reply? We will see.

Chapter 17
Rosemary Leaves my Home

I have to explain this chapter of my life, it is so relevant as to how my life with Rosemary finally starts to unfold and help me towards a new beginning. In the early 70's travelling down a country lane in my sports car at age 29 years old. In the distance a young guy with long hair that resembled a cow boy, crossed the road not straight but diagonal. He seemed to be in deep thought and he was oblivious of my person. I knew at that moment that is the man I am going to marry. I knew even though it was extreme. It's bizarre that is the guy for me. Although we had never met, I never forgot that person that day.

Back to where I am coming from, mid 90s on a Saturday in September, I woke up that morning feeling light hearted for no reason. My business appointments finished midday and while walking home with time on my hands I decide to venture to the gentleman's club. It being ladies day, I grab a gin and tonic and say why not. There was a snooker match being played and this stunning guy approached me who apparently had paid for my drink and We looked at each other and the chemistry, wow. My mind raced, is this my cowboy from thirty years ago? The unbelievable long hair gone but I could never mistake that walk. We were never to be parted from that day on. I never mentioned the country lane because what's the point? We have found each other. I left for home with a spring in my step, phone number in hand, and his last words were phoning me, I am here for you. What a difference a day makes. I feel a women after all the years that I have suppressed my inner self.

However my feelings were soon to be dampened. Rosemary arrives not too worse for wear, "Where is the new found boyfriend you are so smitten with? A word of warning, you are my wife, it will not do you any favors."

My reply was "Your secret cross-dressing is ok, why be so concerned about a little attention given to me?"

A real male younger than him was giving me attention. Were the tables turning? The encounter of meeting after all these years has blown my mind away, of course we have a long way to go, it is not going to happen overnight. Could it be god answering my prayers? I thought yes, I have his phone details. I am putting it to rest as I need time to ponder once. I take that step forwards there will be no turning back. The chemistry is predominate to a point of ache. Rosemary can feel his days are numbered, and was coming somewhat violent. He is paranoid. When the phone rings, the plugs are pulled away from the sockets, furniture thrown, trying to control a male/ female personality is now beyond my comprehension, I am scared, flabbergasted and bewildered. Having tried everything to elevate the situation I find myself in fear of my life. How could a person have such a change of personality? The answer is simple, I am leaving his cocoon. No more loyalty and his long kept secret finished, he will soon be told in no uncertain words you will leave my home and live the life. You have always craved for a two up and down manageable house and now he can cross-dress and drink all the hours available. He did leave my life with a smile on his face, he can now live his life peacefully and accept his problem. With my cowboy love of my life, we eventually married in America, cowboy country, we ride a Harley Davidson and we live abroad, still like new lovers.